Claire Booker

The Bone that Sang

Indigo Dreams Publishing

First Edition: The Bone that Sang
First published in Great Britain in 2020 by:
Indigo Dreams Publishing
24, Forest Houses
Cookworthy Moor
Halwill
Beaworthy
Devon
EX21 5UU

www.indigodreams.co.uk

ISBN 978-1-912876-39-6

British Library Cataloguing in Publication Data. A CIP record for this book can be obtained from the British Library.

Designed and typeset in Palatino Linotype by Indigo Dreams.
Author photo by Ingeborg Siegert
Cover design from artwork by Jane Burn.
Printed and bound in Great Britain by 4edge Ltd.

Papers used by Indigo Dreams are recyclable products made from wood grown in sustainable forests following the guidance of the Forest Stewardship Council.

For Caroline Oliver (1953-2018)
– a generous and loving friend.

CONTENTS

The Bone that Sang 5

Abdul Haroun Almost Medals at Dover 6

A Paving Stone Fights for Freedom 7

At Risk Child 8

Street Cleansing 9

Board Man 10

Stone-whisperers 11

Passion at Oberammergau 12

Leaning Tower, Pisa 14

Empire State Building 15

Racewalker 16

Tree House 17

At the Bear Sanctuary 18

Ivory 19

Student Clinic 20

Passing It On (or Genesis 5 revisited) 22

All Hallows' Eve 23

Deadline 24

Rock Beast 25

Galia Melons 26

Ode to a Pomegranate 27

Baby Blue 28

Double Bass 29

Nightfall at Skiathos Harbour 30

Amma-ji Goes On Haj 31

Life Support 32

View from the Gibralfaro, Malaga 33

The Bone that Sang

After the Grimm's fairy tale

A herdsman, driving his beasts through the torn
mesh of forest, stumbles on a thread
of human vertebrae,
crafts its frail ivory into a mouthpiece,
and a note comes fluting from his lips – its pitch at first
inaudible as the cries of pipistrelles.

In his palace, the generalissimo hoists the ripe meat
of genocide onto his shoulders – builds a cage
from the contortions of his own mouth,
where he constructs truths that walk and talk
like real children.

Ravines clot with secrets. Whispers float
like thistle seed to all corners of the kingdom. He plucks
each chalk-white petal of paperwork
before he signs: *she loves me, he loves me not,*
he loves me, she loves me not.

Under this vaporizing sun, people suck on pebbles
to assuage their thirst.
Men are turned to firewood, children drop like leaves.
But still he knows, how the vanished can fruit
death caps from any scrape of earth.
That bones sing when they find a ready ear.

Abdul Haroun Almost Medals at Dover

The Athletes' Village leaves much to be desired,
but there's no lack of enthusiasm. It's a steeple-chase
over 31 miles. Haroun's been practising hard –
from the bloody sands of Sudan to the concrete beds
of Sangatte. He's out of the blocks at nightfall
hurdling security gates with a gazelle's grace;
dodges surveillance cameras as if they're bullets –
that's been a useful training – then it's a steady race
along the track with the breath of family behind him.
Pace-setters hurtle past at 100 mph, sipping lattés
as they read the latest. At 28 miles he hits the wall.
No podium for Haroun, though he heard the Brits
love an underdog, went wild when two plucky pigs
hot-footed it off a knackers' truck to freedom.

NOTE: *Abdul Rahman Haroun was intercepted in the Channel
Tunnel attempting to seek asylum in the UK.*

A Paving Stone Fights for Freedom

Nothing's touched me
but people's feet, fag ends, vomit,
the shimmy and shine of Monsieur's machine
with its whirling dervish of brushes –

the tiny bones of me
crushed into a relentless formula
which states: *You are this. You remain this.*
You will not change.

And now these iron hooks.

Watch me fly from a boy's grip,
shooting the stars as I did when silica thrashed
melamine in outrageous heat before
worlds were truly set.

Uniforms are fisting a hard stink
on the street. The mob is riffing, cracking
open the sky. Here comes the woooosh of me,
carbon against carbon. Undersides are up!

At Risk Child

Kelly wasn't born to float –
the girl who felt-tipped her body

into a butcher's diagram of cuts;
turned her teeth into installations: metal braces

sprocketed with magnets and paper clips;
who acted out the unthinkable

with Barbies of all colour and creed – forever
snatching at the impossible.

Now that her baby's been taken away,
she's planning another.

Remembers our day in the park
when the ball rolled out of reach. Her face fraught,

ploughing the railings.
Time for a lesson in patience; on how to float

above the must haves? Kelly wasn't born
to float. She rifled the recycle bins for kill, dragged

curtain track across tarmac, pronged it through.
Flat on her belly, arm at full tilt,

the ball came skipping back
on a nest of litter, leaf mould, a child's lost sock.

Street Cleansing

Let us be forensic,
like the ornithologist
who tweezers owl pellets
for clues on the health
of a population –

/bottle/shards/
/flattened/cans/
        /rags/back/pack/
/crushed/bones/

of a homeless man
processed out of the warmth
of a recycle bin
into a Biffa lorry, then
hydraulically compressed.

This bolus
needs careful unpacking.

Board Man

School tipping-out time: wild   shrieks,
bodies heave and break,   buggies scythe
through, dodgem-style.   Outside Pound-
land, a human (self-assembled) positions
himself against the railings.   His limbs
are wood. His hands are rivets.   Beard
full. Anorak copious over dhoti. Placard
pinioned in his solar plexus so the weight
of the big idea   won't put his back out:
BILL'S DINER   ALL YOU CAN EAT
WINGS ON SUNDAYS. Human loop-
hole in the bye-laws,   your eyes   are
hazardous to our indifference.   Perhaps
you're dreaming of kite-flying. Suicidal.
Praying. Performing a C-section in your
head. Or perhaps   you are calculating
the   inflationary   price of   freedom.

Stone-whisperers

It's a neat operation,
earning front page in the Gazette –
Gang Steals Valuable Pavements.
Whole streets have walked, folded
in fleece, packed on pallets then trucked away.
A century of footfall skimmed: imprints
of hobnail, flappers' heels, fag-end burns,
hop-scotch, trikes, drunks, the herringbone
of lovers' feet all untimely ripped
along with flag and sett.

This stone's been filched before –
delver crouched in quarry pit, listened
for a quickening of natural fault, rived out
hidden form, older than the first push
of Alpine peaks. Now it's winched again,
on the swindle, whilst we kerb-skip to detour,
barely note the grunt and guts of it. Hard gold
cretaceous: withstands time and weather,
but not these stone rustlers' jemmies.

They'll be down your way tomorrow, stealing
history from under your feet.

Passion at Oberammergau

Judas Iscariot hangs himself twice weekly,
plus alternate Sundays, which he finds gruelling
even when on form.

Today he's swabbing feet,
scalpel ready to excise pus, while the other Judas
(a butcher by trade) makes with the rope.

Ninety years ago Iscariot was a panto Jew,
branded with the sins of his tribe. But then came Auschwitz
and he's bloomed on guilt.

He pockets the silver, but in his heart
the question burns. Where would you be without me?
Still lathing wood. Hanging out with fisher folk.

Instead, you get to be an Aryan boy
with party tricks: releaser of doves, up-turner of tables,
the ultimate Houdini.

*

Now is the hour when the Magdalene weeps.
He remembers the lush of her hair,
its illicit cascade.

His wife is on stage, belly-deep in Holy Spirit:
blue cloth, ecstasy of being chosen,
separate beds.

He longs to tell her how a man engulfed
in purity becomes bewitched by his own dark stain.
He should have been an angel like their boys –

tableaux vivants brocaded in gold,
their slender trumpets held in absolute stillness.
How easily a man curses free-will after the event.

*

Crucifixion is a laborious business.
Time enough for a beer at the Passionstheater
while he waits to collect his sons.

Simon Peter, whose rise from coward
to Pontiff will be meteoric, stands the first round.
They're joined by Opa, who tells (for the umpteenth time)

how plague returned to the village in 1940
to the tune of moral hatches battening down; everyday folk
secretly burying their ethics against better times.

No chorales that year. Only night screeches,
cattle trucks – his cousin hidden in a hay loft,
half starved, half Jewish,

half in love with the cowman's daughter.
Then the cock crowed and one more conscience
found itself spur-deep in chaff.

*

Tomorrow, he'll betray again with a kiss.
Cheek will touch cheek and a great love will be traded.
He takes the word *forgiveness*; pins it to his chest.

NOTE: *The villagers of Oberammergau in Bavaria, have staged a Passion play every ten years since 1633 (except in 1940). Major roles are shared by two actors who perform the 6 hour play in the Passionstheater throughout the five month festival.*

Leaning Tower, Pisa

There must have been high-fives in heaven
before the pratfall.

This exquisite faux pas has been fuck, fuck,
fucking up since Diotisalvi gave it earthly boots –
his concept of divine proportion
brought to its knees by the raw truths
of clay, aquifers and gravity.

Perhaps because they know how it feels
to have the ground kicked from under them,
people pour into the Piazza dei Miracoli
with their own small bruises. One man's hubris
is another's must-see.

From the lake of bodies, heroes rise up
onto bollards, attempt to rescue
flawed divinity – palm held against blank air,
iPhone carefully positioned so it splints the wound
via the miracle of parallax.

SNAP a would-be caryatid holds the tower
        like a new-found lover.
  SNAP twin girls, palms supine, waitress
          their pile of glistening pillars.
    SNAP just for the kids, Dad buttresses the skew
            with the tip of his furled umbrella.
      SNAP *I'm sick of holding up falling masonry*
              say a wife's timed-out eyes.

Angels and apostles look down in marble
from the pristine Baptistery –
their line of perspective unknowable.
It will take a caul of steel, 600 tonnes of lead
and 30 million euros to tilt the tower
one degree closer to true.

Empire State Building

No-one in my family has been this naked before.
It's terra incognita – areolas floodlit
against brash night, a gale whipping my pudenda.
I'd pinch myself, but I've only got a shaky grip,
what with the 1,000 foot drop
and the size of my butt. Every inch of me
(and that's some) is howling: Let go of NOTHING!
A chopper, just feet away, reels out a boom.
In the down-draught, my landing strip stands to attention
and that's when I see him –

King Kong (miniscule and bipedal)
drumming my mons pubis to the rhythm of
pa paa, pa paa, pa paaa, pa pa pa, pa paa, pa paa, paa, paaa.
I could murder a Kia-Ora. Instead he hands me
binoculars. I pan across the glittering needles of Manhattan
to discover it's a stitch up – I'm being relayed
full frontal in Times Square with the strap-line:
SHOCK SIDE-EFFECT OF CHILLI PEPPERS.
Sue the mothers! squeals Kong from base camp on my midriff,
but my attorney's already in my ear, telling me how
chillies leave me puffy at the best of times:
Go easy on the Jalapeños – last night was off the Scoville scale.

Before I know it, KK and I are endorphined up in
Bloomingdales, slurping noodles until our lips smack.
He reprises his scraper-top climax on the pepper-grinder
and throws me the love-look.
My eyes become saucers, dinner plates, soup tureens . . .
How can I tell him I already fill two floors
and he's the size of a beetle?

Just when I begin to think this could all be a dream,
Hitchcock cameos past with a platter of oysters.
What are the odds?

Racewalker

If you skinned him, he'd show a web of bone.
No fat, just legs pistoning along the cliff.
They'll tell him soon how long she's got.

I never loved her. But it's still eating me up.

Daily, he cracks her breasts in the pan as he fries eggs.
Meets her again in the peeler's rhythmic flick.
Raw white potato. Incised flesh.

Careful - not so near the edge!

Chalk has taken a heavy bite of blue.
Storms send great chunks crashing down –
blind space always in front of him.

She was bad last night. You need your mind to race.

This year he came eighth, third the time before.
He used to win in Belgium against Europe's best.
Still clocks 12k a day; twenty the week ahead.

Never do the full fifty before a race –
you'll only frighten yourself. Best not to know
what you're up against.

Tree House

It's what I remember. His foot twisted back. Like he was
asleep.
Nothing else. Except a trickle of red from his nose.
I let him climb. I shouldn't have.
You worry
yourself sick about gangs. But that?
You couldn't dream it up.
The silence.
That's what got me. Like he was asleep.
No-one warns you.
Trees everywhere: a man crushed on the top deck
at Angel,
that girl at Kew, even over his grave . . .
Ornamentals they called them, cracking their branches,
hissing,
closing in like a pack. When my fist of earth hit
Stevie's coffin
they went ballistic –
shaking,
grinding, pelting, ranting, fat, red, bloody hands
belting down
call yourself a mother, call yourself . . .
suffocating his flowers, shovelling under
his eyes.
You couldn't dream it up.
They've given me a window on the park. It doesn't open.
When I get out,
I'll go to Shetland. Not a single tree on Shetland.
Just sky.

At the Bear Sanctuary

old friendships are respected:
Attila is cohabiting with a wolf.
Florentina waits for Boris by the
perimeter fence, happy to crop
grass under his blinded eye as he
eviscerates oranges (his favourite
fruit) or licks speciality ice cream
made of supermarket throw-outs.
Maria has been breaking hearts
since she arrived – wears her blunt
claws   and   honey   fur
apologetically, treads the same
small circle round the clock. She
used to ride a unicycle in tight
rings inside a larger ring. One
night in Bucureşti she sat down
bare-faced in the sawdust –
refused the crowd's adulation.
Fellow artiste, Max, has turned
solo; rotates on his huge haunches
and paw-claps groups if he spots
them by the fence. He's under his
own management now, perfecting
applause . . .

Ivory

Because it's the colour of fine churned butter,
buffalo milk, chiseled teeth of Xhosa girls.

Because it's hard as the click of Kikuyu on the tongue,
pliant as river fish under the blade.

Because through its bone, saints transubstantiate,
heroes find the whites of their eyes.

Because it has no smell but the stench of Dollar

they track its spoor through acacia bush,
AKs cocked for flare of cool grey swaying flags –

the way each vein flows translucent
to the bed of the ear.

Later, they'll leave her on the red edge
of the Okavango river,

huge docked head, drooling flies.

Student Clinic

Mrs Nkumbo sits astride our scrutiny
in a burst of canary yellow crépe de chine.
Her pleats are impeccable.
Her collar starched to meringue stiffness.
Perched on her head, a hat
which at any moment may burst into song.

Mrs Nkumbo's eyes are calm shades of brown.
They reduce us to specks:
white coats, white faces in eager rows.
We are the brass buttons which hold her in.
Her handbag watches us from the floor
with its gold, bright clip.

Mrs Nkumbo answers questions
with a gush of wit, a gurgle, a lyre bird's call;
graciously lets us chew
on her delicate pathologies. We learn
that she has carried six children in the extinct
uterus beneath her hands.

Mrs Nkumbo owns a full set of tonsils,
wisdom teeth and haemorrhoids – red rags to our bull.
This will be her moment of posterity.
We probe our quarry:
Do they itch? Interrupt evacuation?
Disturb intercourse?

Mrs Nkumbo's smile
is a lizard's walk on hot sand.
Her back flattens its thoracic curve.
Her chair becomes a throne from which to observe
a dozen pairs of supplicant eyes crying out
for sacrifice.

Mrs Nkumbo uncrowns herself,
bestows her hat with reverence to the seat.
Court shoes turn behind the screen,
soft smudge of feet, then rustling,
splashes, latex snap.
She is instructed to turn on her side.

Mrs Nkumbo's silence is a vast and shoreless lake.
We gape like fishes on a slab of ice –
take note of findings, differentials, sequelae.
Nearly done now, Mrs Nkumbo. Nearly done.
On the chair, her hat is a blazing sun
that never sets.

Passing It On (or Genesis 5 revisited)

My mother received hers
from my grandmother, who received hers
from Mama Eyrole, who received hers
from the Count's illegitimate daughter, who received hers
from the pretty laundress, who received hers
from the 12 year old wife of a wheelwright, who received hers
from one unbroken relay of mitochondrial DNA,
with a starting block 5,000 generations back
to a line of fleet-footed daughters
rooting seven branches of Europe on African savannah –
Jasmine, Tara, Ursula, Helena,
Katrine, Velda and Xenia – who received theirs
from the first, great untoppled matriarch.

My hand still holds their traces
in faint outline –
like a Lascaux palm-print of blown ochre.

All Hallows' Eve

Honey will tempt them – they have a sweet tooth.
Be careful not to break the peace
with boiled cabbage or pour water outside
the house.
Leave windows wide open –
even your doors. Talk only of them, as you might
a baby or new lover.
If a spoon drops, leave it there.
Remember, there is much you have forgotten too:
the raw edge of a smile,
how it feels to be looked at with that kind of love.
No need for introductions, they have you
in common.
Give them space to dance –
they'll whirl their shadows round the room,
stretch time to its thinnest.
Your empty chairs will beguile them.
Let them lose themselves in the pleasing shine
of linen and tableware; the niceties
of salt. What does it matter if their glasses
never drain, their plates remain stubbornly heaped?
They have things to tell you.

Deadline

When all else fails, I turn to St Jude
with an inventory of the desired miracle:

annual statements, consolidated tax vouchers,
certificates of deduction of tax

with (from memory) the ominous addendum
a duplicate statement will not normally be issued.

They're holed up somewhere in the house
inside a green folder (how hard is that to spot?)

Kneeling in the under-stairs cupboard,
I grapple with boxes, tennis rackets, old papers,

my mother's last walking stick.
Even her waxed shopping bag gets up-ended –

a handkerchief
drops onto my hand like a dove.

It smells of her.

Rock Beast

Look up long enough
and the cave flips into a Manhattan skyline,
date palms dripping fruit, a clipper's prow bursting
out of lumps of calcite.
Children on ledges
gasp up at the never-ending ribcage,
grip rails
on arrowed paths, attempt to whoop
                          into the vast suck of it.
Their astonished cries
          roll and fade like bee-hum
                    through the cave's great maw.
          This is no time for metaphysical conjecture.
At each corner, people snap flying buttresses
organ pipes   hag faces
the whole gothic shebang,
hesitate at the underbelly – its loops
of moraine like villi of some monstrous gut
endlessly digesting itself.
          Space fills
                    and empties, hauls itself out
in long hard cords.
Skull-boulders, garlanded with light bulbs,
flicker and gurn
as they did that first time, when five *conquistadores*
skipped school, struck a match,
set blaze new worlds.

NOTE: *The caves of Nerja were discovered in 1959 by five schoolboys.*

Galia Melons

Pumped up like amorous frogs,
they bob on beds
of straggled green, brightening
the transit to the airport.

From the seat in front, a small voice
whoops: *Look, footballs!*
This is the land of Don Quixote,
after all, where myth patrols beyond
the *ventana de emergencia.*

In my head, I'm off the bus,
itching to kick. The soil, blood orange,
soft under its baked carapace.
My foot sunk among leaves: broad
hearts on twisted tow ropes –
a ripe globe, nested in the tangle.

I take my maiden penalty under
the pan-hot sky. There it sails,
light as denial, a second sun, blazing
high above the earthen pitch.

Ode to a Pomegranate

You sway that deep navel
like a pout – bright omega, rounder, riper
than the rest.

This gully between us,
hacked back to bare rock, fills with the cries
of mating cats.

What if you plunge –
spill yourself pointlessly into the cove,
will fish be the ones to taste you?

Or shall I wake
to my balcony with its view of five islands,
clouds hung from pine clusters like exotic blooms,

to find you plucked –
youths, sly monkeys scaling branches,
their tongues inked with your purple?

Do not split or spoil.
Your unblemished loveliness will rinse
me of old age.

Baby Blue

It's the rope end of night.
A single bed's no affidavit when you hit thirty.
She heads downtown,
where it's a snake pit of charmers.
Let's see which way this'll swing.

They taxi to his. He sheds skin.
She sheds inhibitions
about starting over, taking risks.
He makes up for shortcomings with heavy grinding
into the polyester wool mix.

The tequila's still talking,
so he Scarlett O'Haras her up the stairs
to the big brass bed,
where he's a rattler 'til daybreak;
her nethers raw and sequined with scale.

All she wants is a soothing bath,
but he's back, butt-naked, one foot on the tap,
with a Fender Dreadnought,
strumming his signature aubade:
It's all over now, Baby Blue.

Double Bass

They make a strange pair –
he, fine boned, dicky-bow, washed-out smile;
she, shellac hard, in-your-face fact,
squeezing him out with her extravagant needs.
She pays the bills, after all.
Each day he must pluck and cajole for hours
(six on concert nights).
He accepts the callouses of tough-love,
strives to recapture that first stir of her ebony neck
with its delicate scroll like a Benin bust,
when his fingertips fizzed
along unexplored borders of her lips,
trekked the polished dunes of her spine.
Some nights, when the moon is right,
the mellow of her breath is an incantation.
He unwraps her tenderly. She peels him to the bone –
takes him soaring on wild harmonic thermals,
her gut in thrall to his bow's impetuous
wing-beats.

Nightfall at Skiathos Harbour

Along the drag an old man sets up his telescope:
look at the moon, see Venus, very cheap.

And there they are – heavenly bodies stripped
to their detail.

From here, islands sink like giant turtles.
Water cascades over ice,

my ouzo blurs from clear to milky.
Venus again, bright but tiny, then lost to cloud.

How you both would have loved this –
sipping the evening with its rhythms splashed

across the bay, these singing trees, the hilltop villas
lighting up like advent.

If I could swap, I'd cross the Styx with whatever coin,
leave behind this air worn lightly.

Just as your bodies conjured mine from night,
so I'd return the favour – trade myself

for one of the silver bream
foraging harbour ink, to feel your footsteps

by the water's edge,
and leap for pieces of your broken bread.

Amma-ji Goes On Haj

We only know that she is far
on her night journey, tiptoeing up each star
in her white sari, ever closer to the Scorpion's sting.

Soon she will forget how
she worked cotton into peacocks and palm trees,
slipped us secret generosities in envelopes.

Those feet that felt nothing for forty years,
will step onto the crescent moon
and dance to the great heartbeat of the Brahmaputra.

On its broad lap, boats are sailing away
with her treasures – six children, the man who was her hearth,
the flame and spark of it,

and prayer –
five wellsprings of the struggling day in which to dip
an ailing body.

Soon she will bathe in the light
of ninety nine moons, her worn wrists with their gold bangles
grown lithe again.

She, who knew only four walls, will dive in the ten directions.
She, who knew the names of fifth cousins,
will know only one name –

the Ka'bah finally within fingers' reach.

NOTE: *Amma-ji means dearest mother/mother-in-law in Bengali.*

Life Support

How you feasted on nature programmes, Amma-ji,
took your bed travelling

to the fierce expanses of Antarctica.
The Emperor penguin on his egg: if it broke

we'd watch him warm a smooth, round rock instead.
Now they tell us you've been dead all week –

that your lips twitch from intubation,
your fingers grip mine out of primitive habit.

I tell them: go, let me incubate my rock.

View from the Gibralfaro, Malaga

Here, where Caliphs wove empires –
only the call of swifts

breakfasting above burnt ochre crenellations
that steam like washed horses.

From this height, the city's noise
pools at its ankles.

There are tower blocks, cranes, cement silos,
a cruise liner in its rectangular bath.

A tiny bicycle cuts a stubborn line
along the Avenida de Toros.

In the old town, the cathedral exposes its back –
red, shrunken, almost shameful.

Hill-top churches spread north like a painted Belén.
Even the tips of the sierras seem touchable.

I can see almost everything,
except you.

Today, you'll lay your head in the well-turned soil
of a Surrey morning.

The quiet truth of you
breathed out in snowdrop and celandine.

Acknowledgements

Thank you to the editors of the following publications in which these poems (or versions of them) first appeared:

Abdul Haroun Almost Medals at Dover, View From the Gibralfaro, *The Spectator*; Deadline, At the Bear Sanctuary, *Poetry News*; Racewalker, *Structo*; Tree House, *The New Welsh Reader*; Ivory, Baby Blue, *The Interpreter's House*; Life Support, Passing It On, *Stand*; Stone Whisperers, *Prole*; Passion at Oberammergau, A Paving Stone Fights For Freedom, All Hallows Eve, Ode to a Pomegranate, Nightfall at Skiathos Harbour, *Poetry Salzburg Review*; Amma-ji Goes on Haj, *The High Window*; Double Bass, *The Frogmore Papers*; Board Man, *Ambit*; At Risk Child, *South Bank Poetry*; Student Clinic, Galia Melons, Empire State Building, Leaning Tower, The Bone That Sang; *Magma*.

My gratitude to Dean Atta, Lisa Kelly, Jane Maker, Alan Price, Marion Tracey and Caroline Vero for their fantastic support and feedback. Thank you also to all at Original Poets, the Brighton Stanza Group, Rottingdean Writers' Group, Loose Muse and Pier Poets.

Last, but not least, my sincere thanks to Dawn Bauling and Ronnie Goodyer for choosing to publish these poems.

Also by Claire Booker

Later There Will Be Postcards
(Green Bottle Press, 2016)

Indigo Dreams Publishing Ltd
24, Forest Houses
Cookworthy Moor
Halwill
Beaworthy
Devon
EX21 5UU
www.indigodreams.co.uk